Contents

Origins and early locomotives

It could never work. If the steam locomotives themselves did not explode, the passengers' heads would do the same when exposed to speeds of 30mph. Such were the sceptics' views when the first steam locomotives came on the scene in the early 19th century.

But take a look at steam's origins and it's easy to see where the cynics were coming from. Ask people about the first steam locomotives and many will say "Stephenson's Rocket". But it was Richard Trevithick, a Cornish engineer, who pioneered the modern steam locomotive. Trevithick developed stationary steam engines. Alarmists were horrified when one of these, a stationary pumping engine at Greenwich, exploded in 1803, killing four men. In fact, this was a watershed moment. Realising the inherent dangers in high-pressure steam, Trevithick incorporated two safety valves in future designs, one being a lead plug located in the boiler just below the safe water level. If the water dropped to a dangerous level, the plug was exposed, and with the cooling effect of the water lost, the lead melted and the plug came away, releasing the pressure. This feature remains basically unchanged to the present day.

Trevithick pressed on and in the same year he built a steam-powered road coach, called the London Steam Carriage. Then, on 21 February, 1804, the steam locomotive on rails was born. Trevithick had built a stationary engine to drive a hammer at the Pen-y-Darren Iron Works near Merthyr Tydfil in Wales. Encouraged by the works' proprietor, Samuel Homfray, the engine was mounted onto wheels and its piston connected to cogs to drive the wheels.

Homfray made a bet with Richard Crawshay, owner of the Cyfarthfa Iron Works, for 500 guineas, that the locomotive could haul 10 tons of iron along the normally horse-operated Merthyr Tydfil Tramroad for 9.75 miles from Penydarren to Abercynon. Hauling five wagons containing the iron and 40 men, Trevithick's locomotive successfully completed the journey in four hours and 5 minutes, at an average speed of nearly 5mph. Some of the rails – designed only to hold horse-drawn wagons – broke under the locomotive's weight, but the bet was won and the steam locomotive was truly born.

A similar locomotive was built for the Wylam Colliery in Northumberland, but again the locomotive broke the wooden rails and Trevithick went back to the drawing-board. In 1808 he exhibited the locomotive "Catch me who can" on a circular track at Bloomsbury in London. The locomotive attained speeds of 12mph but once again was too heavy for the track and public interest proved limited. Disillusioned,

The expansion of railways soon saw the network spread well beyond the major cities

Trevithick lost interest in locomotives and subsequently concentrated on developing stationary engines. Sadly, he died penniless and alone in 1833 – but Trevithick's legacy as the pioneer of the steam locomotive is immense.

Inspired by Trevithick, John Blenkinsop, the manager of Brandling's Colliery, at Middleton, near Leeds, decided to use a steam locomotive for use on the colliery's existing wagon way. In 1812 the engineer Matthew Murray built the "Salamanca", the first successful twin cylindered locomotive. Blenkinsop believed that an engine light enough to operate successfully would not generate sufficient adhesion, so he incorporated a rack and pinion system. The Salamanca featured an "extra" centre cogged wheel which locked into a rack standing just outside the 4ft gauge tracks. Thus Blenkinsop invented the rack railway, as used by many mountain and sleep incline railways around the world to this day. Not only that, the Middleton Railway was the world's first commercial railway to be operated by steam locomotives. The railway still exists as a standard gauge heritage railway, with a wide range of very unusual steam and diesel locomotives, and it is well worth a visit.

Meanwhile, George Stephenson, a young engineer born in Wylam and working on the colliery railway there, had been inspired by the brief appearance of Trevithick's locomotive there and, in 1813, William Hedley and Timothy's Hackworth's Puffing Billy, which operated successfully on the line. Puffing Billy is the world's oldest surviving steam locomotive and is exhibited at the Science Museum in London. In 1814, Stephenson built his first locomotive, "Blücher", which had flanged wheels to help keep the locomotive on the track and cylinder rods directly connected to the wheels.

Much early steam developed on small industrial lines, such as the Corris Railway

Stephenson went on to build the Hetton Colliery Railway, opened in 1822. Around the same time, businessman Edward Pease was preparing the Stockton and Darlington Railway, to link coal mines in the area to Stockton's port. Pease intended the railway to be horse-drawn, but Stephenson persuaded him to at least try some steam power – at this time most people were still sceptical as to whether locomotives, which were still very slow and unreliable, could supersede equine haulage. Stephenson built "Locomotion No 1", which, when the line opened 27 September 1825, hauled the first steam-hauled passenger train. It was something of a makeshift effort, with most passengers sitting in coal wagons and one experimental coach.

Initially the Stockton and Darlington Railway was a somewhat chaotic affair, with both horse and steam traffic operating. After a few years it became apparent that steam locomotives were faster and much more powerful. In 1833, the railway became purely steam operated, with timetables, double tracks and primitive signalling. And with the gauge of 4ft 8 _ inches that was to become standard, it established the template for modern railways.

By 1829, George Stephenson's next major project, the Liverpool and Manchester Railway, was approaching completion.
This was a much more ambitious undertaking – a 35 mile line with the 2,250 yard Wapping Tunnel beneath Liverpool, followed by a 2 mile cutting, a nine span viaduct at Sankey Brook Valley and the crossing of Chat Moss bog, achieved by sinking wooden and heather hurdles into the mire until it could support the rails.
In October 1829 trails were held at Rainhill to determine whose locomotives would operate traffic on the line. There were five entries, and "Novelty", built by John Ericsson and John Braithwaite, astonished the crowds by reaching speeds of 28mph, but mechanical problems meant it had to drop out. Timothy Hackworth's "Sans Pareil" performed with credit and despite suffering a cracked cylinder was bought by the Liverpool and Manchester Railway, where it served for two years. But the winner was "Rocket", built by George Stephenson and his son, Robert, the only locomotive to complete the trials without any mechanical problems.

Rocket is sometimes mistakenly seen as the first steam locomotive – it wasn't, but it did include several innovations that set the standard for modern engines.
Most notably, Rocket had a multi-tubular boiler, greatly improving efficiency.

The Llangollen Railway was opened in 1865

The railway bandwagon was soon well and truly rolling. Not only did railways prove much more efficient at transporting goods than canals, the demand for passenger traffic was much greater than expected. Railways looked a rock-solid investment – speculation in them became rife and as with all technological booms, the earlier caution about their feasibility evaporated.

In addition, while the government took an interest in safety matters for the operation of railways, its approach to the construction of lines was very much laissez-faire. There was no nationwide plan to develop a railway network as we know it today. The "Railway Mania" simply resulted in a plethora of separate schemes. By 1843, the number of railway miles in England, Scotland and Wales topped 2,000, and in 1845 "The Times" reported that over 600 new lines were proposed.

As the railways grew, some companies grew faster than others, and took over smaller lines to expand their own network. One of these was the Great Western Railway, whose first major route was from Bristol to London. The company's chief engineer was Isambard Kingdom Brunel, a fearless innovator. Never afraid to be the maverick, Brunel decided to use a gauge of 7ft 0 _ inches. Brunel argued that the standard 4ft 8 _ inches adopted by most railways was simply a carry-over from the

mine railways and that broad gauge would provide for faster, more comfortable and, of course, more spacious trains. Despite the spread of standard gauge elsewhere, Brunel was not a man to be cowed and he pressed on with broad gauge tracks and rolling stock – although the Great Western eventually had to give way, in 1892, to the spread of standard gauge. Brunel appointed Daniel Gooch, aged just 20, as superintendent of locomotives. Brunel and Gooch founded the locomotive works at Swindon, from where came the first engines setting the Great Western's reputation for distinctive chrome green liveries. The most unusual engine produced by Gooch was an "underground" locomotive for the Metropolitan Railway linking Paddington and Farringdon Street, the first underground railway in the world, opened in 1863. Gooch's special class of 0-2-4 tank engines were curious creatures – squat and broad because of the 7ft gauge and fitted with condensing tanks for the exhaust, so that it was not discharged into the tunnels.

Steam locomotives elsewhere made rapid strides towards the look associated with modern times. In 1861, the Stockton and Darlington Railway completed a route across the Pennines to join the London and North Western at Tebay. For this, engineer William Bouch built two superb locomotives, the "Brougham" and the "Lowther". With a 4-4-0

wheel arrangement, they were the first bogie, four-coupled engines to run in Great Britain. And while drivers formerly were cruelly exposed to the elements, Bouch added a huge closed-in cab – something that proved surprisingly unpopular, and many engines continued to have no cabs for several years to come! One of Bouch's locomotives, the NER "100" Class 0-6-0 No 1275 survives and is exhibited in the National Railway Museum at York.

Engines were getting stronger and faster – and the competition was intense. The late 19th century was marked by the "Race to the North", where rival railway companies would literally race each other from London to Scotland. A serious derailment at Preston in 1896 brought an end to racing – but by now the steam locomotive was a beast of speed. And more speed meant more revenue.

George Jackson Churchward, the Chief Mechanical Engineer of the Great Western Railway, began to deliver a series of locomotives of which led the way in design and innovation. One of the earliest was "City" Class 4-4-0 "City of Truro", built at Swindon in 1903. On 9 May, 1904, while hauling the "Ocean Mails" special from Plymouth to London Paddington, City of Truro was recorded to have reached a speed of 102 _ mph on the descent between Whiteball Tunnel and Wellington in Somerset. The achievement has always been disputed – partly because feelings about reckless speed chasing were running high at the time and the figure was not publicised for another three years. Also, the figure was recorded by just one timekeeper, Charles Rous-Marten and it has been suggested that he became carried away in the excitement. On the other hand,

Rous-Marten, a writer, was a leading authority on train speeds.

City of Truro remained in service until 1961, hauling special excursions in the latter years and was subsequently displayed at the National Railway Museum as a static exhibit. It was restored to working order in 1984 and in 2004 a £130,000 refit was completed.

Steam locomotives had become much faster than anyone had anticipated. Invariably there were some accidents – but in 1906-07 there were three mysterious tragedies that highlighted the dangers of reckless speed.

On 30 June 1906 a boat train run by the London and South-Western Railway, and headed by a Drummond 4-4-0 "L12" class, left Stonehouse Pool

The Somerset and Dorset Railway came into being in 1875

The preserved North Norfolk Railway was part of the Midland and Great Nortern Joint Railway, fromed in 1893

at Plymouth just before midnight. At the time there was intense competition between the London and South-Western and the Great Western Railway for high-class liner traffic and the boat specials ran at high speed into London. The driver of the train took his charge through the curve east of Salisbury at greatly excessive speed – he was travelling at around 70mph – and a destructive derailment ensued in which 28 people died. As the dead included the driver and fireman, the cause was never fully explained, but it is most likely that the driver simply did not realise the level of danger.

The Great Western Railway was developed from 1833 onwards

Much more mysterious was the accident that followed soon after, on 9 September 1906 at Grantham on the Great Northern Railway. The 8.45pm passenger and mail train from King's Cross to Edinburgh, headed by a brand new Ivatt Atlantic, No 276, and driven by an experienced driver, failed to make its scheduled stop at Grantham, passing several signals at danger and then taking a subsequent junction at too high a speed. The train derailed and was badly wrecked; 14 people died, including the driver and fireman. The cause has never been remotely ascertained and Tom Rolt, in his book "Red For Danger", called the accident "the railway equivalent of the Marie Celeste". Naturally, all sorts of wild theories were put forward, such as that the driver had some kind of seizure – yet the signalman at Grantham saw both driver and fireman calmly looking forward in the cab.

A year later there was a strikingly similar accident, again with a night passenger train, this time at Shrewsbury on the London and North-Western Railway. On 15 October 1907, the driver of a train from Manchester, instead of slowly down to stop at Shrewsbury, where the approach included a very sharp curve, came tearing through at 60mph – the train was derailed and 18 people died. Needless to say, the three accidents had a negative impact on public opinion and it was to be some years before railway companies felt they could publicly boast about speed.

When World War One broke out in 1914, the government took control of the railways, through a Railway Executive Committee, who in turn relied on the managements of the many existing rail companies. The strain on the railways was immense. They were not physically shattered, as they would be in World War Two, but demands fell on the railways for which they were totally unsuited.
The railway network had been developed to meet regular peacetime needs; by and large the companies knew what sort of, and what volumes of traffic to expect, and if there were changes, they had chance to prepare. But now some companies were put under intense pressure. For example, the London and South Western Railway served the military centres of Aldershot and Salisbury Plain, plus Southampton and its docks. During the war it carried 20 million soldiers, 7 million of whom passed through Southampton docks. The South Western took on this responsibility alone.

After the war, some companies were, quite simply, worn out. Nationalisation was discussed but met strong opposition by traditionalists. But even the latter conceded that if the railways were to remain under private ownership, changes would have to be made. The compromise solution thought best suited to further development was to have fewer companies.

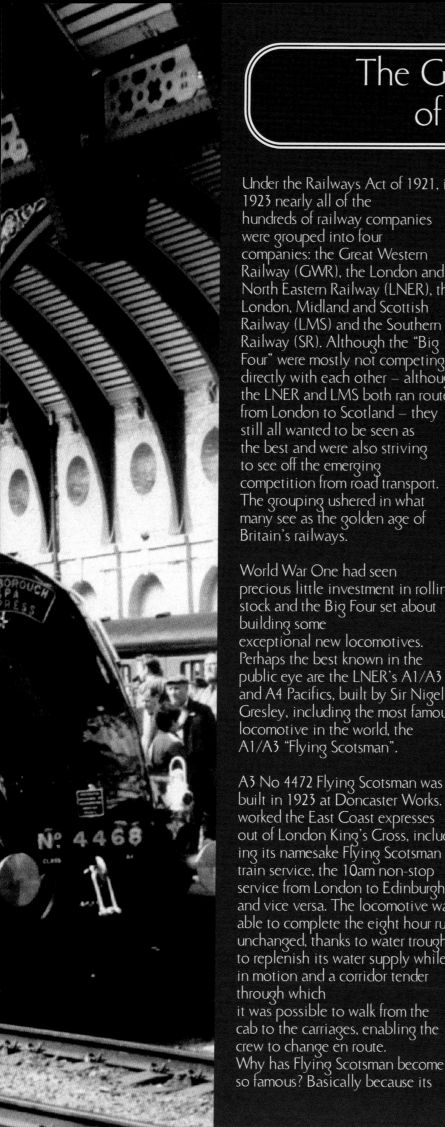

The Golden Age of Steam

Under the Railways Act of 1921, in 1923 nearly all of the hundreds of railway companies were grouped into four companies: the Great Western Railway (GWR), the London and North Eastern Railway (LNER), the London, Midland and Scottish Railway (LMS) and the Southern Railway (SR). Although the "Big Four" were mostly not competing directly with each other – although the LNER and LMS both ran routes from London to Scotland – they still all wanted to be seen as the best and were also striving to see off the emerging competition from road transport. The grouping ushered in what many see as the golden age of Britain's railways.

World War One had seen precious little investment in rolling stock and the Big Four set about building some exceptional new locomotives. Perhaps the best known in the public eye are the LNER's A1/A3 and A4 Pacifics, built by Sir Nigel Gresley, including the most famous locomotive in the world, the A1/A3 "Flying Scotsman".

A3 No 4472 Flying Scotsman was built in 1923 at Doncaster Works. It worked the East Coast expresses out of London King's Cross, including its namesake Flying Scotsman train service, the 10am non-stop service from London to Edinburgh and vice versa. The locomotive was able to complete the eight hour run unchanged, thanks to water troughs to replenish its water supply while in motion and a corridor tender through which it was possible to walk from the cab to the carriages, enabling the crew to change en route.
Why has Flying Scotsman become so famous? Basically because its

circumstances have always kept it in the public eye. It was a flagship engine for the LNER: it represented the company at the British Empire Exhibition at Wembley in 1924 and carried the same name as the LNER's most famous train, which it often hauled.
On 30 November 1934, Flying Scotsman became the first locomotive to be officially recorded at 100mph – and in stark contrast to City of Truro, this was accompanied by a blaze of publicity.

Flying Scotsman continued to work for British Railways after the nationalisation of the railways in 1948, and for 15 years it sported a darker BR green livery and was numbered 60103. After its withdrawal in 1963 it was immediately sold to railway enthusiast Alan Pegler, and restored to its original livery and 4472 number, became one of the first preserved steam engines to work regular main line traffic, hauling several rail tours.

In 1969, Flying Scotsman travelled to America, and when its backers ran into financial problems, there were fears it could be stranded there. It was eventually saved by William McAlpine in 1973 and return to Britain.

Flying Scotsman now resides at the National Railway Museum in York, who bought it for £2.2m in 2004. It is currently in pieces and undergoing a major overhaul.

While Flying Scotsman has the greatest fame, it is its sister A4 locomotives which are the most dramatic in terms of appearance and performance. Inspired by a visit to Germany in 1933, where he saw

London to Scotland traffic but differences of opinion within the company prevented them pressing ahead with developing express passenger locomotives. It was only when William Stanier became Chief Mechanical Engineer of the LMS in 1932 that more powerful locomotives were built in earnest. Stanier's Princess Coronation Class, introduced in 1937, were the most powerful express passenger locomotives to work in Britain. Initially, the locomotives were streamlined, but its benefits were marginal at best and the streamlining was removed after the war. First out of the works, No 6220 "Coronation", was presented in Caledonian Railway blue. It briefly held the world speed record when reaching 114mph in June 1937. This prompted the LNER to regain the record with "Mallard" the following year. The non-streamlined versions were commonly referred to as Duchesses, and three have been preserved. On The Southern Railway, Richard Maunsell produced his 4-6-0 Lord Nelson express locomotives from 1926 to 1929, and followed these up with the SR Class V or "Schools" class. The Tonbridge to Hastings line had limitations which meant an express locomotive that could operate in some low tunnels and round sharp curves was needed. Maunsell went for a short wheelbase 4-4-0 arrangement, heavily influenced by the existing Lord Nelson design. Forty were produced from 1930 to 1935, all named after public schools, and they are seen as the most powerful 4-4-0s to operate in Britain. One Lord Nelson and three Schools locomotives have been preserved, while the nameplates from six scrapped Class Vs are displayed in their respective schools and colleges.

Charles Collett developed two 4-6-0 express locomotives for the GWR in the 1920s, the "Castle" and King" class. Both types gave excellent service and on 6 June 1932 No 5006 "Tregenna Castle" covered the 77 miles from Swindon

streamlined diesel trains, Gresley decided to apply the same principle to his Pacifics. The streamlined design of the A4s meant that they epitomised the speed, style and grace of the heyday of steam haulage. Furthermore, the first A4 to emerge from Doncaster Works in 1935, "Silver Link", was turned out in silver livery to match its special coaches, giving the train a "space age" look way before the dawn of the space age!

But the A4s were more than just good-looking – Gresley also made several internal improvements to make the locomotives better than the A3s. On 3 July 1938, Gresley's work was rewarded in dramatic style as A4 locomotive "Mallard" set a world steam speed record of 126mph on Stoke Bank, just north of Peterborough.

The other companies were determined not to be outdone. The LMS competed with the LNER for

to London Paddington at an average speed of 81.68mph. The Kings hauled the top expresses right up until the early 1960s and their supporters point out that they were better all round performers than the diesel hydraulic locomotives that replaced them; without doubt, they enjoyed far greater longevity.

Away from the spotlight, smaller locomotives performed the bread-and-butter work of hauling local passenger and freight services. Perhaps the best-loved of the tank engines is the pannier tank, which became synonymous with the GWR's sleepy south-western branch lines. Several versions of this 0-6-0 locomotive were produced, most prolifically the 5700 class, of which 863 were built between 1929 and 1949. The panniers were sturdy and reliable and some would say the best six-coupled engines ever built. They had everything one could ask for from a branch-line locomotive: easy to fire, economical and capable of handling heavy loads.

n addition, mainline freight was a still a mainstay of the network. A 2-8-0 wheel arrangement became the most popular wheel arrangement for freight locomotives. With the formation of the "Big Four" competition heightened for freight as well as passenger traffic and some locomotives were built with exceptional power. Not surprisingly, Sir Nigel Gresley was not to be outdone by anyone and in 1925 he introduced the class P1 three-cylinder 2-8-2 heavy mineral locomotive. These had the same boiler and firebox as the express passenger Pacifics but were also fitted with a "booster" for the second pair of small wheels – an auxiliary engine with additional cylinders which could be used when greater force was required. The booster could increase the locomotive's haulage capacity by 25 percent.

In fact, the P1s were too good! Unless hauling near full loads their coal consumption was uneconomical and the only suitable route for them was to haul

coal traffic between New England Yard near Peterborough and Ferme Park in North London. Therefore only two such locomotives were built.

Another remarkable engine made for power was the 0-10-0 Lickey Banker, built by the Midland Railway in 1919. A banker's sole purpose is to provide extra power on steep inclines by being added to the rear of trains. Conventional locomotives often fulfilled the job adequately, but the Lickey Banker was built solely for use on the 1 in 37 _ Lickey Incline over two miles between Bromsgrove and Blackwell. Known affectionately as "Big Bertha" or "Big Emma", the Lickey Banker provided service for the LMS and British Railways up to 1956. Another colossus of a locomotive, the LNER class U1 2-8-0+0-8-2 Beyer-Garratt, was used for banking coal trains over Worsborough Bank in South Yorkshire. It was also trialled on the Lickey Incline but the trails were unsuccessful and it was scrapped in 1955.

The Second World War

The glamour and colour of the "Big Four" was, literally, erased when war broke out in September 1939. The railway companies were brought under central control, run by a Railway Executive, based at the disused Down Street London Underground station on the Piccadilly Line.

First to go was comfort and speed. All restaurant car facilities were withdrawn, except on the Southern, and maximum speeds were cut to 60mph – the latter was to reduce wear and tear on track and rolling stock. At night, windows were blacked out. Seat reservations were withdrawn, as were some sleeping services. Thus the luxuries of train travel which many businessmen and others had utilised and enjoyed were wiped out in an instant. In addition, trains became much more crowded. First came evacuation, with huge numbers of children sent from the big cities to the country; this was followed by mass mobilisation, with troops and others undergoing military training being moved around.

The progress of the steam locomotive did not, however, come to a standstill. Firstly, the War Office was keen that there should be a supply of powerful freight locomotives, for use both at home and overseas. First came the War Department "Austerity" class 2-8-0, designed by Robert Riddles, of which 935 were built, and then a 2-10-0 Austerity – the first major batch of

ten-coupled locomotives to work in Great Britain. Many locomotives from both classes saw service overseas.

However, style did not completely lose out to function. Sir Nigel Gresley produced a swansong just before his death in 1941 – the V4 class 2-6-2 locomotive. The V4 was a response to the demand to have a versatile mixed-traffic locomotive that could work both passenger and freight on sections of line unsuitable for heavier locomotives. The V4s were beautiful locomotives and were highly thought of. The first, No 3401, was named "Bantam Cock" to emphasise its lightweight design. Its sister locomotive, 3402 was never named but acquired the nickname "Bantam Hen". After Gresley's death and his succession by Edward Thompson, no more V4s were produced, though both worked until 1957.

Meanwhile, Oliver Bulleid, a former assistant to Gresley, became Chief Mechanical Engineer of the Southern Railway in 1937. Bulleid was mainly concerned with producing an improved locomotive for the boat expresses from London to Folkestone and Dover. He was a remarkable character who combined great imagination with the determination to see every project through to its conclusion. He therefore refused to let the war get in the way of

his quest for a "super locomotive" and true to his word came up with the SR Merchant Navy class 4-6-2, which incorporated several innovations. The locomotives gained a characterful appearance, firstly through their "air-smoothed" casings, which were not for streamlining – the locomotives had a flat front end – but to enable them to be cleaned using carriage washing machines. Secondly, they sported Bulleid-Firth-Brown wheels, wheels that gain strength by being a number of box sections rather than having traditional solid spokes. The

locomotives were finished in
Bulleid's own "unique" livery of
vivid malachite green, although
during the war they were
repainted in Southern Railway
wartime black livery. The
Merchant Navy class also
included several mechanical
innovations and luxuries such
as electric lights for the crew
and steam operated firedoors.

The Merchant Navy class was
successful and many of the 30
produced survived to the
closing years of steam on British
Railways. Eleven of these
survive today, though not all of
them have been restored to
working order.

Bulleid then showed himself to
be adaptable to wartime
demands by producing the Q1
0-6-0 freight locomotive. The
Southern, which until the war
was primarily a high density
passenger railway, suddenly
faced demands to transport large
quantities of wartime supplies.
Bulleid produced a purely
functional locomotive which
was the most powerful 0-6-0
steam locomotive ever to
run in Britain. It was powerful,
light and a huge success. Like
the Merchant Navy engines,
the Q1s, affectionately known
as "Charlies", were "air
smoothed" and had Bulleid-
Firth-Brown wheels. They were
also turned out in black, a
colour they retained
throughout their working lives.
The Q1s were versatile enough
to sometimes work secondary
passenger services and
the last locomotive was not
withdrawn until 1966.
Thankfully, one survives,
No C1/33001, currently
at the National Railway
Museum, though it has
spent many years working
on the Bluebell Railway,
where it will hopefully be
steamed again sometime in
the future.

Nationalisation, British Railways and the end of steam

The war left the railway companies effectively bankrupt. On 1 January 1948, the railways were nationalised. It was to spell the beginning of the end for day to day steam railway operation in Britain. In 1954, a modernisation plan was put forward, which included the replacement of steam traction with diesel and electric locomotives. However, the plan was badly executed and ushered in an inglorious and costly period for the railways.

Diesels were rushed into service before they had been fully tested and many proved to be chronically unreliable. For example, the class 28 Metropolitan-Vickers "Metrovicks", introduced in 1958, were all handed back to the manufacturer in 1961 because of engine problems and even cab windows falling out while running! Engine problems continued on their return to service and their bizarre Bo-Co wheel arrangement, with six wheels at one end and four at the other, added to maintenance problems. All 20 locomotives were withdrawn in 1967-68, though one, D5705 luckily survived to eventually be preserved on the East Lancashire Railway, and enjoys a cult following. Compare this with the class "P" steam tank locomotive No 753, who began work on the South Eastern and Chatham Railway in 1909. Its eventful career included work in France, around Folkestone harbour, and under nationalisation, with British Railways as a shed pilot at Brighton. Even after withdrawal in 1961, it was bought to work at a private mill in Sussex before eventual preservation on the Kent and East Sussex Railway.

But it was not only some diesel classes that proved costly failures. Oliver Bulleid, never one to shy away from going his own way, produced a unique steam locomotive which lasted less than two years and ended up as little more than a historical footnote. But Bulleid's "Leader" as it became known, was a brave attempt to extend the life of steam traction by radically modernising it.

Based on his experiences with electric locomotives, Bulleid concluded that many of their advantages could simply be transferred over to steam power. In 1947 construction began of the first Leader, with five in total ordered to be built. The locomotive resembled a diesel or electric in appearance (funnily enough, the class 28 diesel looked somewhat similar to the Leader). It had a cab at each end, enabling dual direction running and eliminating the need for turntables. A corridor connected the cabs and a third cab in the middle from which the fireman worked. The Leader was articulated with two 0-6-0 bogies at each end. The locomotive was entirely encased in steel sheeting, giving it its diesel like appearance, with the idea that it could be washed in modern stock cleaning machines.

The first Leader, No 36001, came out of Brighton Works in June 1949 and immediately began trials that led to its downfall. Despite some impressive runs, several problems came to light. Some difficulties were mechanical – it was suggested that a complete re-design was needed; other problems included the firemen complaining that their cab became very hot – indeed, they usually ran with the cab door open – and it appears that many firemen actually found the conditions intolerable.

The Leader made its last trip in November 1950 and the decision to

scrap the project was made on March 1951. All five Leaders were scrapped, including the incomplete locomotives numbers 36002-5, with £170,000 or more spent on the project. All that remains is number plate 36001, on display at the National Railway Museum. The story of the Leader is examined in detail in three books by Kevin Robertson, most recently "The Leader Project: Fiasco or Triumph?"

Until 1960 regular steam locomotives were still coming out of the works. At first, British Railways decided to produce locomotives based on existing

In 1954, British Railways Standard Class 8 No 71000 "Duke of Gloucester" emerged from Crewe Works. This 4-6-2 locomotive was a prototype for a new batch of express steam locomotives, but did not perform well, mainly due to steaming problems and no more of its type were constructed. It was withdrawn after just eight years and ended up languishing, rotting and forgotten at Barry scrap yard in Wales until a massive restoration effort, beginning in 1973 saw it restored to working order in 1986. During restoration, two basic design faults were discovered: the chimney was too small, resulting in

lines, including climbing Shap bank on the West Coast main line with a heavy load in appalling weather conditions, but with power in reserve. This rags to riches story shows what might have been had history taken a different course.

In March 1960, "Evening Star" emerged from Swindon works – the last steam locomotive built by British Railways. A striking "9F" 2-10-0 express freight locomotive, Evening Star was an impressive performer – so good in fact, that it was also fast enough to operate passenger trains – but lasted for only five years

designs from the "Big Four" – the first priority was to replace worn out stock and get the railways running again. Over 1,500 locomotives were built this way, many for mixed traffic work.

From 1951, British Railways began producing its own standard designs, often looking to LMS practice but also incorporating ideas from else-where. For example, 172 Standard Class 5MT 4-6-0s were built, essen-tially being a development of the LMS' "Black Five", which had proved the most successful mixed-traffic locomotive.

poor boiler draughting, and the firebed air inlet dampers had been built wrongly, causing poor oxygen supply and combustion. No wonder "Duke of Gloucester" had proved "difficult".

With these faults rectified and restoration complete, "Duke of Gloucester" was steamed again on the Great Central Railway in 1986. Four years later it ran with a full load on a main line and was found to be a fantastic performer, producing steam at a furious rate. "Duke of Gloucester" has since performed great feats on the main

before being withdrawn, although it was preserved and is at the National Railway Museum.

Production of the 9Fs only began in 1954, yet 254 were produced. They were, powerful, fast, reliable and economical. Yet their life was shockingly short. Although a few lasted until 1968, the first withdrawals took place on 31 May 1964. These included numbers 92176 and 92177, who had both only emerged from Crewe Locomotive Works on 31 March 1958.

The critics were scathing. Adrian Vaughan, in his memoirs as a signalman, "Signalman's Twilight", writes: "Steam engines were cut up after running only 1,000 miles since undergoing heavy repairs." He adds: "One by one the diesel types arrived: the 'Hymek', 'Brush' and 'Western' classes, all full of manufacturers' promises, all doomed to failure. Some classes were worse in this respect than others but one and all were rescued, when they broke down, by the despised steam engines several of which had, to my certain knowledge, been retrieved from scrap yards."

But the die was cast. Despite the undue haste of modernisation, the arguments in favour of diesel and electric were hard to counter. Steam locomotives needed four hours just to reach working pressure. They were high maintenance, and despite the nostalgic glamour, the job of driving them was a tough one. And diesel and electric was much, much more environmentally friendly.

British Railways chairman Richard Beeching instigated mass closures of unprofitable lines under the "Beeching Axe" of 1963. This made a lot of locomotives redundant and accelerated a process that had begun over a decade earlier. The first victims were some of the more ancient and odd engines that British Railways had inherited from the "Big Four" in 1948. It was only with the modernisation plan that scrapping began in earnest. There were 114 scrapyards involved in the elimination of 16,000 locomotives – including most of the 2,537 locomotives built by British Railways since 1948. Cashmore's of Great Bridge in Tipton, Staffordshire, was the site

for cutting up 1,500 locomotives between 1961 and 1969. This included 219 "8F" freight locomotives – around a quarter of the entire class.

One yard that became an unexpected haven was Woodham Brothers in Barry, south Wales. Here, 213 locomotives were saved for preservation. The Barry story really happened by happy accident. The scrapyard was so busy cutting up redundant wagons that the disposal of the locomotives was put to one side. In the meantime, rail enthusiasts quickly realised that the only source of locomotives for preservation was going to literally vanish once the withdrawn engines were cut up. Over the next two

decades there was a slow but steady exodus from Barry, with the last locomotives, "the Barry ten", not leaving until 1987.

The last days of steam were exhilarating ones for enthusiasts as they sought to see, travel behind and photograph the dwindling number of locomotives. It was often a sorry sight – locomotives were filthy and many had nameplates removed, presumably to keep them from souvenir hunters. As early as 1966, steam was gone for good on the Western Region and on 9 July 1967 it was all over on the whole Southern Region.

By 1968, steam operation was limited to the north-west of

England; locomotive numbers were hovering around the 300 mark and dwindling all the time. The areas around Manchester and Preston were some of the best areas to get a last taste of steam. But locomotives were no longer steamed in Manchester after 1 July and the last sheds to survive with steam were Carnforth, Rose Grove, Lostock Hall and Patricroft. The very last locomotives to survive were mostly ex-LMS Black 5s and 8Fs plus some British Railways standard classes.

The last steam-hauled operation by British Railways is a subject of debate and some mystery. There is no doubt that British Rail ran a rail tour on 11 August 1968, when a special enthusiasts' service ran from Liverpool to Carlisle and back. One of the engines that hauled this, Black Five 4487,1 was the last locomotive in steam at a British Railways depot, at Carnforth on 13 August. But the "real" end for many was the previous weekend, when on 3 August, the last scheduled passenger service ran – the 21.25 Preston to Liverpool, hauled by Class 5MT 4-6-0 number 45318, which reached 78mph at one point. This was certainly the end in terms of scheduled passenger services. Historians who have dug deeper point to "Black 5" locomotive 45212 shunting and providing heating for sleeper carriages into the bay platform at Preston on 4 August and it has also been mooted that Stanier 8F 48519 powered a permanent way train at Rose Grove on 4 August. But, wherever one draws the line, the simple fact remains unchanged: it was all over for regular mainline steam.

Steam locomotive and railway preservation

When the axe fell on British steam it was swift and brutal. People had to act quickly to not only to save locomotives from the cutter's torch but to preserve railways for them to run on. Today the preservation movement is stronger than ever – thanks in the main to countless hours of unpaid dedication and determination by enthusiasts.

Forms of preservation vary – from at its very simplest, a non-operative locomotive mounted on a plinth and left open to the elements and wear and tear from those who climb aboard it, right through to steam locomotives operating on a fully-timetabled railway open to the public year round. There are many shades of grey between these two – for example, some railway centres store locomotives – sometimes out of the public eye – which they work on restoring as a hobby over many years while occasionally steaming working engines over a short stretch of track. In contrast, steam-hauled special trains nowadays often run with a full rake of coaches over long stretches of the mainline network.

The earliest form of preservation, however, was in museums. In 1862 the Science Museum acquired George Stephenson's "Rocket", and railway preservation was born. Today, Britain's premier railway museum is the National Railway Museum in York – home to over 100 locomotives, 200 items of rolling stock and numerous associated exhibitions. It opened in 1975 when it combined collections from the existing York Railway Museum and the British Railways collection in Clapham. Steam locomotives at the National Railway Museum range from pioneering colliery locomotives to the last locomotive built for British Railways, "Evening Star". Unusual exhibits include a replica of a Great Western broad gauge Iron Duke locomotive and Southern

Railways' 4-6-2 Merchant Navy class "Ellerman Lines", which has had its body partly cut away so that visitors can see the "insides" of a locomotive.

There are many other museums and railway centres dotted around the country. Some, such as Didcot Railway Centre, and Barrow Hill Roundhouse and Railway Centre in Derbyshire, are sited in former locomotive sheds. Others cater for more esoteric tastes, for example, Astley Green Colliery Museum in near Walkden on the outskirts of Manchester, which houses the largest collection of colliery locomotives – mainly underground mine engines – in the United Kingdom.

But if you want to ride behind live steam, the best place is a preserved railway. The world's first railway preservation society was that involved in saving the Talyllyn Railway in the 1950s. But it was the Beeching Axe and the end of standard gauge steam that ironically ushered in a new golden age – that of railway preservation.

Standard gauge preservation was pioneered by the Middleton Railway, but the first ex-British Railways line to be saved was the Bluebell Railway in East and West Sussex. The line originally ran from East Grinstead to Lewes but in 1954 – well before Beeching – its closure was proposed, and this took place the following year. However, the closure was hotly contested and historically it set precedents that helped buy time to save other lines in the future. When the railways grew in the 19th century, lines were authorised by Acts of Parliament, which imposed a legal requirement on the owner to provide some sort of regular service. Shortly after closure, a local resident, Madge Bessemer, discovered that the Acts of

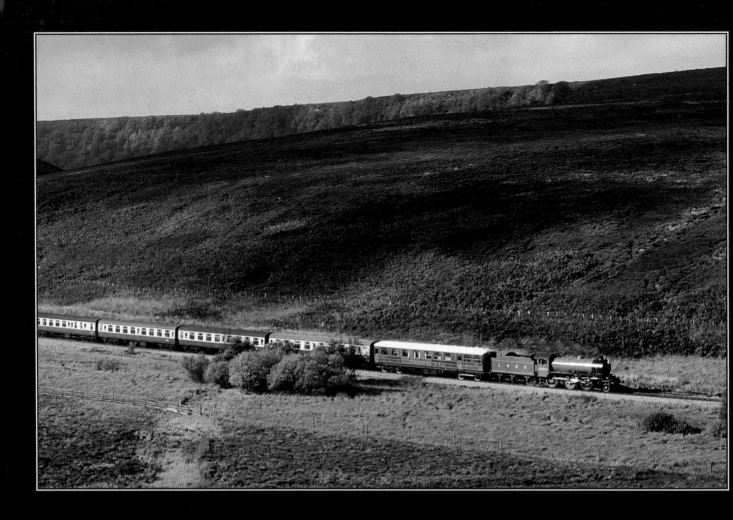

1877 and 1878 pertaining to the East Grinstead to Lewes line required "four passenger trains each way daily to run on this line daily with through connections at East Grinstead to London and stop at Sheffield Bridges, Newick and West Hoathly". The Act needed to be repealed before services could cease and British Railways was forced to re-open the line in August 1956 with what was nicknamed a "sulky service" or "spite service" as the trains ran with just one carriage and stopped only at the stations nominated in the Act. The Act was eventually repealed and the line closed in 1958 – but vital time had been bought. The Bessemer Arms pub at Sheffield Park on the Bluebell line is named in Madge Bessemer's honour.

After closure a group of enthusiasts stepped in to save and re-open the five mile section of line between Sheffield Park and Horstead Keynes. The line has subsequently been gradually extended northwards and is now on the final push northwards to re-connect with the national rail network at East Grinstead. The

extensions have been fraught with difficulties as the tracks had been lifted and reverted back to other uses in the hands of private landowners.

The latter illustrates the urgency that confronted preservationists in the 1960s. Steam had taken a double blow – first modernisation, and then the Beeching Axe, closing many rural lines. There was no room for sentiment at British Railways – their priority was to scrap locomotives, close the lines and lift the tracks. This has been one of the subsequent criticisms of the period – namely that lines were obliterated with undue haste rather than being "mothballed", that is, closed and left more or less intact pending possible re-opening.

The North Yorkshire Moors Railway is a classic example of a "Beeching" line that has been saved and since gone from strength to strength. The second longest heritage line in Britain, it is the 18-mile Pickering to Grosmont section of the former Whitby-Pickering-Malton route. The line was purchased following its closure in 1965 and the North

Yorkshire Moors Railway Historical Society at first concentrated on keeping the line alive, with various open days and steam galas. By 1973 a timetabled service was up and running and the railway has not looked back. Trains run every day from April to October, plus on many other days in the winter and the line draws on a wide range of steam and diesel locomotives. The working steam is mainly mainline locomotives from the "Big Four" and British Railways. The line connects with the national network at Grosmont and in 2007 through trains began running on sections of track beyond Grosmont.

Preserved lines were originally conceived purely as "heritage railways" to save steam and other locomotives in running order. The next step in their evolution was to run timetabled services as a tourist attraction – vital for revenue. Recently, some railways have taken things a step further and attempted to provide a "working" passenger or even freight service. The Wensleydale Railway in Leeming Bar and Redmire is one such line.

The vast majority of trains are operated by diesel multiple units, though BR standard class 4 tank locomotive No 80105 hauls several summer services. The Weardale Railway in County Durham also attempted to provide a commercial service but – with 36 full-time staff employed at one point – it ran into massive financial problems, although it has survived.

In May 2007, the Severn Valley Railway used a steam locomotive to haul a train of 50 water pipes for Severn Trent Water to the Trimpley water treatment works. Although this was a one-off, it shows how far heritage railways have evolved from the early days of being groups of enthusiasts armed with little more than hope and determination.

Steam locomotives hauling special trains on the main lines have also become increasingly common. After the demise of mainline steam in 1968, British Railways initially imposed a total ban on steam operation. This lasted until 1972 – one could say allowing for a sufficient period of mourning – before steam specials were allowed to run on a limited basis. Traffic has grown steadily since and has become big business. There are now some regular summer steam services on main lines – for example, the Scarborough Spa Express, running every Tuesday, Wednesday and Thursday throughout the summer. The turntable at Scarborough, which was destroyed and filled in the early 1970s, was excavated and restored in 1981 to facilitate turning steam locomotives.

Steam preservation has not reached its conclusion. Heritage lines continue to be extended and new lines and railway centres opened. And there are still steam locomotives awaiting restoration – the rush to save condemned engines during the 1960s and 1970s means that many are still a "work in progress" or simply awaiting the many, many hours of work, expertise – and serious cash – needed to bring them back to life. For example, on the Pontypool and Blaenavon Railway, here are six ex-Barry Scrapyard

GWR locomotives in need of complete restoration. Two ex-Barry locomotives, Bulleid Merchant Navy Class 35011 "General Steam Navigation" and LMS Hughes Crab Class No 4258 are even thought to be privately stored near Binbrook in Lincolnshire, some distance away from a railway line. Some enthusiasts favour the idea of actually building new locomotives from scratch rather than trying to revive hulks that have been stripped and left open to the

elements for nearly 40 years.

Could some steam locomotives even be hidden away, like a treasure trove awaiting re-discovery for future preservation? Children's fiction author the Reverend W Awdry, famous for his Railway Series of books, used such a theme for the book "Duke The Lost Engine", where a railway is closed and one of its engines, "Duke" stored in a shed which becomes overgrown, only for "Duke" to be discovered years later and restored. Such an idea is so romantic that it has undoubtedly planted seeds of hope among some enthusiasts. Today, this mainly

centres on the idea that the government could have a "strategic reserve" of steam locomotives kept in hiding for use in case of a national emergency. Supposed locations for such "hidden engines" include Box Tunnel near Corsham, a rumour fuelled by military underground facilities nearby and an adjoining tunnel formerly used for a quarry railway. Speculation has also centred on a Ministry of Defence depot at Heapey in Chorley – with

no evidence – and MOD Longtown in Scotland, where redundant diesel locomotives have undoubtedly been stored down the years.

As any such steam locomotives would almost certainly be unusable, and with the Cold War over and the government having since revealed the whereabouts of, or even sold, much more sinister things – nuclear shelters, for example – than some old locomotives, it sees likely that such ideas are born purely of wishful thinking or those who have fun making up stories, but the myth will doubtless live on among those determined to perpetuate it.While

Industrial standard gauge steam

While steam may have died as a mainline hauler in August 1968, standard gauge locomotives were seen operating on private working railways for at least 18 more years, maybe more. Industrial standard gauge steam locomotives are perhaps the least celebrated but they were amongst the most hard-working and durable.

By nature industrial steam shies away from the limelight. The locomotives work on private lines usually well away from the public eye and a designed purely for function – there was no need to make them pleasing to look at. Yet it is for these very reasons that the industrial locomotive holds a curious fascination.

Let us not forget that it was industrial lines that saw the steam locomotive's birth – more specifically, the colliery railway. The "railway mania" also saw an expansion of colliery lines. Colliery complexes owned their own stretches of track and sidings for the shunting and preparation of coal trains. In these cases it made sense for the lines to operate on standard gauge tracks, as the lines could then connect to the main network and the wagons be transported to various destinations by main line locomotives belonging to the big companies.

Collieries used their own locomotives, which may well conjure up images of odd antique engines trundling around the yards. In fact, the production of steam engines for colliery and general industrial use continued late into the steam era and included some of the last innovations to be applied to steam. The Hunslet Engine Company of Leeds began producing its Hunslet "Austerities" in 1943 and continued to build new locomotives as late as 1964. With a 0-6-0 wheel

arrangement, the Hunslet Austerities were classic shunters – powerful, robust, simple and with wide route availability. They were first built for War Department use in World War Two, which helps explain their name, synonymous with the time. When the National Coal Board was created in 1947 it adopted the Austerity as its standard shunter and 77 new Austerities were built for this purpose between 1948 and 1964. With production of locomotives continuing into the 1960s, the later Austerities were fitted with an Austrian Giesl ejector multiple blast pipe, which greatly reduced the engine's coal consumption. With the Clean Air Act of 1956, the second innovation was a complex modification which almost eliminated the locomotives' output of black smoke.

The Hunslet Austerities continued to work beyond the end of British Railways steam in 1968 and were still a common sight in the 1970s. A handful even made it into the 1980s, with Cadley Hill Colliery and Bold Colliery among the places still using steam locomotives. Their use became more and more sporadic but locomotives were still being steamed at Bold Colliery well into the 1980s – the last industrial steam locomotive to remain in service at a colliery was an Austerity that was taken out of service at Bold Colliery in 1984. But it was not the last standard gauge steam locomotive to be used in the UK for anything but enthusiast purposes. For example, a 0-4-0 saddle tank was used on a regular basis at Falmouth Docks until August 1986 and there are other sketchy or unsubstantiated accounts of industrial steam lingering on elsewhere. Austerity WD198/WD98, "Royal Engineer" was in Ministry of Defence ownership and regularly steamed at Long Marston until being withdrawn in 1991 – the last operational steam locomotive owned by

the Army. The latter is preserved on the Isle of Wight Steam Railway and the locomotive from Bold Colliery also survives and is named "Sapper" on the South Devon Railway and restored to its original War Department livery. Hunslet Austerities have proved popular with heritage railways and around 70 examples have been preserved.

Docks, harbours and shipyards were a haven for industrial steam. Again, standard gauge was ideal to connect to the main network, but the dock environment often required locomotives that could deal with tight curves and narrow clearances. The B7 0-4-0 saddle tanks, which originated on the Lancashire and Yorkshire Railway in the late 19th century, were ideal for the job. Known affectionately as "pugs", they weighed just 21.25 tons, had a wheel base of 5ft 9 inches and wheels of 3ft diameter. Pugs had several unusual features to help them work well in the dock environment, such as protective covers on the slide bars and a smoke hood on locomotives that worked in warehouses, in

order to deflect the blast from the chimneys. Two pugs have survived, including number 51218, which works on the Keighley and Worth Valley Railway.

William Doxford and Son's shipbuilding yard at Sunderland used steam crane locomotives to lift weights up to 4 tons. Their use lingered on until 1971 and incredibly, no less than four examples survive in preservation.

Some of the oddest-looking industrial locomotives were built by the Sentinel Waggon Works at Shrewsbury. While most steam locomotives were developed and built in isolation and thus retained the basic original design features, Sentinel specialised in construction steam-powered road vehicles and transferred some of its developments into the latter area into its locomotives. The Sentinel used a high-pressure vertical boiler and was a late attempt to radically develop the steam shunter in the face of the rise of the diesel. Indeed, at first glance the later Sentinels can easily

be mistaken for diesel shunters.

Another departure from the mainstream came from Aveling and Porter of Rochester, a manufacturer of traction engines and steam rollers. They also transposed their road designs to rail and their locomotives were not far removed from being traction engines on rails. Thus they were characteristically very slow, being able to muster little over 8mph, but proved powerful and gave good service in industrial use. "Sydenham" who can be seen at the Buckinghamshire Railway Centre at Quainton, worked in Erith from 1895 until 1953.

Fireless locomotives were a remarkable innovation. They were designed for use in areas where fires were prohibited for safety reasons; for example, in chemical works or munitions factories. The locomotives worked by having a steam reservoir which was fed from an external source; the locomotive then worked on the stored steam until the pressure dropped to a minimum level, after which it was re-charged.

Andrew Barclay and Sons of Kilmarnock were experts at producing small, simple locomotives and they built 114 fireless locomotives between 1913 and 1961. Several have been preserved but the locomotives are rarely operational because of their low power and problems with steaming them away from their natural environment. However, the Buckinghamshire Railway Centre has achieved the feat of steaming one of its fireless engines, which formerly worked for the Laporte chemical manufacturers in Lancashire. Laporte assisted the society with the locomotive's restoration and it was charged by using steam from another locomotive.

Fireless locomotives could make a comeback because of their ability to use steam generated from elsewhere, notably using solar power. Fireless locomotives are low maintenance, efficient and easy for drivers to operate.

Great Little Trains

Narrow-gauge steam railways offer a unique fascination. Although most now solely run as heritage railways, they remain little altered since their working days and thus provide a true journey back in time.

A narrow-gauge railway is any line with a track gauge narrower than the standard 4ft 8 _ inches. At their zenith there were over 1,000 narrow gauge railways in Britain, and their significance cannot be overstated.

Richard Trevithick's first steam locomotive ran on narrow gauge tracks and the Middleton Railway was 4ft gauge. The subsequent setting of a standard gauge did anything but diminish the growth of narrow-gauge railways. On short industrial lines there was no need for the railway to conform to the standard of neighbouring systems. Narrow gauge was economic and lines and engines could be built to cope with sharp curves and, of course, confined spaces. The locomotives that were built were

supplies. These demands led to the construction of characterful locomotives that have won the hearts of thousands.

Most narrow gauge locomotives with 0-4-0 or 0-6-0 wheel arrangements but some real oddities also emerged, such as the Fairlie 0-4-4-0 locomotives used on the Ffestiniog Railway. These are double-ended locomotives with two boilers, two chimneys, two sets of cylinders and so on, and therefore capable of being driven equally well in both directions – the latter idea was taken up again in the design of most mainline diesel and electric locomotives. Also distinctive are "coffee-pot" vertical-boilered locomotives pioneered by De Winton & Co for use in the Welsh slate mines.

Indeed, it was north Wales that saw the narrow-gauge boom. The demand to carry large quantities of slate over short distances in difficult terrain was perfect for narrow gauge.

and was the first narrow-gauge railway in Britain to do so.

Elsewhere, narrow-gauge railways were built to carry freight: stone, clay and metals. Others, such as the Lynton and Barnstaple Railway in Devon, opened in 1898, were passenger railways to connect small communities with the main line network. Narrow-gauge railways continued to flourish well into the 20th century, but then the triple blow of improved road transport, the economic crisis of the 1930s and the Second World War took its toll. Many lines closed.

Shortly after the war, Tom Rolt, an engineer, author, idealist and railway enthusiast, stumbled across the Talyllyn Railway in North Wales. The Talyllyn, with a gauge of 2ft 3 inches, was opened in 1865 to serve the Bryn Eglwys slate quarry. It also carried passengers and survived, unchanged and almost unnoticed by the outside world, through both World Wars. By the 1940s the line was in a much neglected state with just one working locomotive and an unreliable, sporadic service. The quarry had closed and the railway only continued to operate because of the benevolence of its owner, Liberal politician Sir Henry Haydn Jones. Haydn Jones vowed that the railway would survive as long as he did – so when he died in 1950 the line was plunged into an even deeper crisis and it appeared that it would close. However, Rolt had by now been inspired and had other ideas. He banded together a group of enthusiasts who restored the line, a story recounted in Rolt's classic book "Railway Adventure". The Talyllyn was the first British railway to be run entirely by volunteers and was the prototype for railway preservation. Both the railways original locomotives, "Talyllyn", built in 1864, and "Dolgoch", from 1866, have survived and still operate traffic.

Several other narrow gauge steam railways are running today. They include the aforementioned Ffestiniog Railway and the Lynton and Barnstaple Railway. The latter was closed in 1935 but saw a short section re-opened in 2004 after much

designed for being able to work economically over short distances – robust, relatively easy to steam, maintain and operate and with only limited capacity for coal and water

In 1863, the Ffestiniog Railway, with a gauge of just 1ft 11 _ inches, switched from horse-drawn to steam traction. Two years later it introduced regular passenger traffic

work by enthusiasts.
Another notable line is the 2ft
7 inch rack-and-pinion Snowdon
Mountain Railway, opened in 1896.
It is the only steam operated rack
railway in Britain. Starting at
Llanberis, the railway ascends 7.4
miles to the peak of Mount
Snowdon, the highest peak in Wales.
The gradient is as steep as 1 in 5.5 in
many places. There are two operational intermediate stations and all
trains currently terminate at one of
these, Clogwyn, as the Summit
station is closed until the spring of
2008 because of construction work.
The railway uses a mixture of steam
and diesel traction, with four
operational steam locomotives, three
of which are original engines from
1895 and 1896, when the line
opened. The locomotives have
inclined boilers, so that the boiler
tubes and firebox remain submerged

when on the gradient. The
locomotive always runs chimney first
up the mountain pushing a carriage
in front of it – the carriage is not
coupled to the locomotive. The
journey to the summit takes around
an hour, at an average speed of
5mph. The line is open from late
March to early November. The
steam trains running through the
spectacular mountain scenery makes
for an unforgettable experience and
needless to say the railway can get
very busy in high summer..

Miniature railways differ from
other narrow-gauge railways in
that they use locomotives that are
scaled-down replicas of standard-
gauge locomotives. Nearly all such
lines were built purely as tourist
attractions and several use diesel
locomotives with a mocked-up
steam locomotive exterior.

A notable exception is the
Romney, Hythe and Dymchurch
Railway in Kent. With a 1ft 3 inch
gauge, it runs for 13.5 miles from
Hythe to Dungeness and uses
steam locomotives mostly modelled
on those from the Golden Age of
Britain's railways. The Romney,
Hythe and Dymchurch railway was
financed by millionaires
Captain J E P Howey and
Count Louis Zborowski and
opened in 1927.
It was not built as a novelty but as a
public service and has maintained
that principle to this day. Although
heavily reliant upon tourism, the
Romney Hythe and Dymchurch
Railway is still used to transport
school children year round, during
school terms. In the past the railway
has also transported fish and
uncrushed shingle and still
occasionally carries parcels.

On the footplate

The life of the engine driver has been romanticised and much dreamt of. For many who drove locomotives it was "just a job" – but one that carried with it pride and prestige. It was also tough – and sometimes dangerous.

Being an engine driver in the early days had little in the way of romance. The locomotive cab was open – a situation at its worst in tunnels when drivers and firemen were engulfed in smoke. It was not into one's eyes. But advancing civilization has removed that disadvantage. A snug shelter is now provided for the driver: an iron partition arises before him, with two panes of glass through which to look out. The result is that he can maintain a far more effectual look-out; and that he is in great measure protected from wind and weather."
Indeed, conditions gradually became better for engine drivers, but it remained a tough profession.

passenger train at Uffington but hitched a lift on a light engine running up line towards Reading. It was running tender first but he gave no thought for the inhospitable conditions and climbed aboard. The engineman carried him off at Didcot, frozen stiff, and he died later from the effects of exposure."

Fifty years on, despite considerable advancements in technology and comfort, engine driving was still a demanding job. In 1962, Vaughan rode on the footplate from London Paddington to Pembroke Dock. "The noise in the cab... was deafening at 20mph. Over the extensive junctions passing Old Oak Common at 50mph I thought that the concussions racking the engine were more than metal – or flesh and

unknown for drivers to be overcome by asphyxiating fumes.

As AKH Boyd wrote in his "Recreations of a Country Parson", published in 1862: "In departed days, when the writer was wont to stand upon the foot-plates, through the kindness of engine-driving friends now far away, there was a difficulty in looking out ahead: the current of air was so tremendous, and particles of dust were driven so viciously particularly in winter. Adrian Vaughan, in "Signalman's Twilight", writes: "Make no mistake, travelling thus was a very serious matter with the temperature well below zero Fahrenheit and Swindon an hour away. In the winter of 1909, I remember being told, Bert Vaughan was a porter-signalman at Faringdon. He was a young man from Henley and one weekend was very anxious to return home. For some reason he would not wait for a stopping blood – could stand.

"As we approached Slough at 70mph, Dai yelled to me to stand with him in the centre of the cab. 'There's a bad lurch over the Windsor junctions, it'll smash your head against the cabside if you stand in the corner there... Then came the lurch. I had never experienced anything like it and its horrific viciousness took my breath away. The engine heeled over left and right, not like a ship might, but savagely and suddenly as if the engine were falling over a cliff. There was a crash that drowned the usual racket and I felt fear sweep through me as my mouth went dry. The tender followed the same course, whipping over as if it was going to break away and an avalanche of coal rattled down onto the footplate."

On a few occasions work on the footplate became a real matter of life and death. There have been countless heroic acts, some that have passed unrecorded and unmentioned, but four drivers and fireman have been awarded the George Cross for acts of extreme bravery when driving a steam locomotive.

Driver Benjamin Gimbert and fireman James Nightall were both awarded the George Cross for bravery when an ammunition train exploded at Soham on 2 June 1944. As the train approached Soham, Gimbert saw that the wagon next to the locomtive was on fire. Realising that the whole train could explode, Gimbert and Nightall decided that they must separate the blazing truck from the rest of the train. Nightall managed to do this and the pair then drove the engine and burning wagon down the line. As they approached Soham signal box, Gimbert shouted to the signalman to stop the mail train which was almost due. At that moment, the bombs in the blazing wagon exploded. A 20ft deep crater was blown in the ground below the track and all the buildings at Soham station were destroyed. Fireman Nightall was killed instantly, and the signalman later died of his injuries. Despite being blown into the air by the explosion, Gimbert survived. During his six-week stay in hospital some 32 assorted pieces of glass, gravel and metal were removed from his body. He lived to be 73, and in 1981 two class 47 diesel locomotives were named after Gimbert and Nightall.

On 9 February 1957 driver John Axon was in charge of the 11.05am freight train from Buxton to Warrington, driving Stanier 8F 2-8-0 No 48188. Axon was preparing to top his heavy 33-wagon train before descending a steep gradient when

the steam pipe feeding the brake suddenly fractured, disabling the brakes. The cab was filled with scalding steam but although Axon was badly burnt he tried to get the train under control with the handbrake. He told his fireman to jump clear and apply as many wagon brakes as possible but the train began to speed out of control. Axon remained at his post, despite the steam and boiling water which was continuing to pour into the cab, and his severe burns. He continued to fight for control of the engine but it crashed into the rear of another freight train and he was killed. In 1981, a class 81 electric locomotive was named in his honour. On 9 February 2007, the 50th anniversary of Axon's death was commemorated when class 150 diesel multiple unit 150273 was named after him.

On 5 June 1965, Wallace Oakes was driving a passenger train near Crewe when the cab was filled with smoke and flames blowing back from the firebox. Despite this, Oakes stayed at the controls and applied the brake. His burns were so severe that he later died, and he almost certainly did so in ensuring the safety of his passengers. Class 86 electric locomotive 86 260 was named after him.

Steam on the silver screen

Several famous and not so famous feature films have featured the steam age as a backdrop. Most films featuring outdoor scenes provide some kind of unintentional historical source – in many feature films it is purely a tantalising glimpse of a busy marshalling yard or main line as a backdrop to a brief scene.

But some films have centred on railway and steam scenes, or at least notably featured them. The most famous is "Brief Encounter" from 1945, the story of an illicit love affair. Starring Cecilia Johnson and Trevor Howard as the furtive couple, much of "Brief Encounter" was filmed at Carnforth station in Lancashire. Carnforth station fell into a very sorry state indeed from the 1970s onwards, but has thankfully been restored, with a "Brief Encounter"

refreshment room and exhibitions. "Oh, Mr Porter!" starring Will Hay, gives a glimpse of the beginning of the decline of the rural branch line. A comedy based on the story of an incompetent railway worker, who due to family connections, is shunted away for the job as stationmaster at the remote station and almost unused station of Buggleskelly in Ireland. The station used for filming in 1937 was in fact Cliddesden, on the Basingstoke and Alton Light Railway, which had been closed to all traffic the previous year, while some of the scenes were shot in the goods yard at Basingstoke. Today, nothing remains of Cliddesden station.

Also dealing with the fate of branch lines, and perhaps of even more interest to enthusiasts, is "The Titfield Thunderbolt" from 1953. Inspired by the volunteers who had recently saved the Talyllyn Railway, the comedy-drama tells the tale of villagers fighting to save their local line from closure – a quite prophetic storyline. Filmed in colour and starring Stanley Holloway, George Relph and John Gregson, "The Titfield Thunderbolt" was mainly shot on the recently closed branch line along the Cam Brook valley in Somerset, and Titfield station was in fact Monkton Combe station. Again, the station is long gone, but the engine that stars in the film, "Lion", survives. A Liverpool and Manchester Railway 0-4-2 from 1838, it was already in preservation at the time of filming and was painted in red and green for the Technicolor cameras. "Lion" is currently exhibited at the Museum of Liverpool.

"The Railway Children", from 1970 made a new departure – using preserved railways to recreate the past. Based on the novel by Edith Nesbit, it was filmed on the Keighley and Worth Valley Railway and in particular its station at Oakworth. Heritage railways have since continued to be an important resource for film and TV directors looking for vintage rail locations and the Bluebell Railway was used for Carlton TV's version of " The Railway Children", filmed in 1999.

Milestones in speed

Year	Railway	Location	Locomotive	Speed	Notes
1808	Private	Bloomsbury	Catch-me-who-can	12 mph	1.
1830	Liverpool & Manchester	Rainhill	Novelty	28 mph	2.
1830	Liverpool & Manchester	Rainhill	Rocket	30 mph	3.
1854	Bristol & Exeter	Wellington	4-2-4T No 41	81.8 mph	4.
1904	Great Western	Wellington	City of Truro	102 mph	5.
1934	London & North Eastern	Essendine	Flying Scotsman	100 mph	6.
1935	London & North Eastern	Essendine	Papyrus	108 mph	7.
1935	London & North Eastern	Arlesey	Silver Link	112.5 mph	8.
1937	London Midland & Scottish	Betley Road	Coronation	114 mph	9.
1938	London & North Eastern	Essendine	Mallard	126 mph	10.

1. Richard Trevithick's demonstration locomotive on a circular track.

2. Built by John Ericsson and John Braithwaite. Reached 28mph, some claim it ran at much higher speeds after the trials. Worked on the St Helens and Runcorn Gap Railway for three years.

3. George and Robert Stephenson's winner of the Rainhill Trials.

4. Broad gauge engine designed by James Pearson.

5. Stop watch reading. Claimed to be the first steam locomotive to reach 100mph.

6. Recording equipment in dynamometer car momentarily registered 100mph – has been disputed by railway historians.

7. Sister engine to Flying Scotsman. First fully authenticated, documented and undisputed run at over 100mph. Tragically, the locomotive was scrapped.

8. First LNER class A4 locomotive. Broke all previous records on its inaugural journey.

9. Coronation class, set new speed record on a press run.

10. Holder of world record for steam locomotives.